Especially for

....

From,

....

Date

....

My Prayer JOURNAL

Peaceful Moments to Bless Your Heart

BARBOUR BOOKS
An Imprint of Barbour Publishing, Inc.

Published by Barbour Books, an imprint of Barbour Publishing, Inc., P.O. Box 719, Uhrichsville, Ohio 44683, www.barbourbooks.com

Our mission is to publish and distribute inspirational products offering exceptional value and biblical encouragement to the masses.

Member of the
Evangelical Christian
Publishers Association

Printed in China.

Introduction

* *

*I urge, then, first of all, that petitions, prayers,
intercession and thanksgiving be made for all people —
for kings and all those in authority, that we may
live peaceful and quiet lives in all godliness and
holiness. This is good, and pleases God our Savior,
who wants all people to be saved and to
come to a knowledge of the truth.*

1 TIMOTHY 2:1–4 NIV

As women living out our faith in an increasingly busy world,
it's so important to spend time each day in the peaceful
presence of our loving Creator. *My Prayer Journal: Peaceful
Moments to Bless Your Heart* is a collection of prayer starters
and scripture selections designed to help you set aside daily
quiet time and soak in the heavenly Father's peace-giving
presence as you begin a purposeful
conversation with Him. As
you read through the prayers
and meditate on the scripture
selections, journal your own
prayers and praises in the
generous space provided.

Be blessed!

Strength to Forgive

Lord, give me the strength to forgive others so You will forgive
me my own trespasses. When someone offends me, remind
me of the great grace You have poured out upon me so that
I may be gracious as well. In Jesus' name I pray, amen.

....
....
....
....
....
....
....
....
....
....
....
....
....
....
....
....

*Give us today our daily bread. And forgive us our
debts, as we also have forgiven our debtors.*
MATTHEW 6:11–12 NIV

Purpose Revealed

Heavenly Father, I pray that You will transform my
mind and show me Your will for my life. When Your
purpose is revealed to me, Father, help me to accept
my responsibility and do Your will. Amen.

*Do not conform to the pattern of this world, but be
transformed by the renewing of your mind. Then you
will be able to test and approve what God's will is —
his good, pleasing and perfect will.*
ROMANS 12:2 NIV

Wise with Finances

Thank You, Lord, for the abundant life You have blessed me with. I may not always have a lot financially, but I am so blessed and happy in Christ. Help me to be wise with what money I have and to use it in a way that pleases You. Amen.

"To those who use well what they are given, even more will be given, and they will have an abundance. But from those who do nothing, even what little they have will be taken away."
MATTHEW 25:29 NLT

Trust

Lord, I thank You for Your guidance and protection day after day. Although I never know what the day will bring, You have a plan for my life and I choose to trust in You. Amen.

....
....
....
....
....
....
....
....
....
....
....
....
....
....
....
....

Trust in the LORD with all your heart and lean not on your own understanding; in all your ways submit to him, and he will make your paths straight.
PROVERBS 3:5–6 NIV

Make My Home a Blessing

Lord, I want my house to be Your house—a house of prayer, a place of comfort and peace, a refuge to those in need. Just as I give of my money and time, please help me to be a good steward of this structure I call "home." May my home be a blessing to all who pass through its door, whether they are here for a short visit or a longer stay. I want to honor You as I use my home for Kingdom work. Amen.

Who can find a virtuous and capable wife? She is more precious than rubies. Her husband can trust her, and she will greatly enrich his life. She brings him good, not harm, all the days of her life.
PROVERBS 31:10–12 NLT

Wisdom and Guidance

Jesus, my Wonderful Counselor, I ask for Your wisdom
and guidance. Instruct me in the ways that I should go.
I trust that You will guide me so I may serve
You all the days of my life. Amen.

*For to us a child is born, to us a son is given, and the government
will be on his shoulders. And he will be called Wonderful
Counselor, Mighty God, Everlasting Father, Prince of Peace.*
ISAIAH 9:6 NIV

Sing Praises

I praise You, Father, from the mountaintops—when things go well. It is easy there! But in those times when things go wrong, help me to praise You still. Give me the faith to praise You from the valleys of my life. You are sovereign, and all of Your ways are perfect. Amen.

. . . .

. . . .

. . . .

. . . .

. . . .

. . . .

. . . .

. . . .

. . . .

. . . .

. . . .

. . . .

. . . .

. . . .

. . . .

. . . .

. . . .

I will give thanks to you, LORD, with all my heart; I will tell of all your wonderful deeds. I will be glad and rejoice in you; I will sing the praises of your name, O Most High.
PSALM 9:1–2 NIV

Blessing Others

Lord Jesus, draw my family close to You. Fill our
home with Your presence and our lives with Your
love. In turn, help each one of us to realize the
importance of blessing others. Amen.

*"But who am I, and who are my people, that we should be able
to give as generously as this? Everything comes from you,
and we have given you only what comes from your hand."*
1 Chronicles 29:14 niv

True Forgiveness

Heavenly Father, show me the way to true forgiveness. Help
me to forgive as I have been forgiven. It is not always easy,
but it is always Your will for me in Christ Jesus. Amen.

*"For if you forgive other people when they sin against you, your
heavenly Father will also forgive you. But if you do not forgive
others their sins, your Father will not forgive your sins."*
MATTHEW 6:14–15 NIV

For All Things. . .

Thank You, precious heavenly Father, for giving
us all the things we need for life and godliness.
You are Jehovah-Jireh, the Great Provider. Amen.

....
....
....
....
....
....
....
....
....
....
....
....
....
....
....

*And because of his glory and excellence, he has given us great and
precious promises. These are the promises that enable you to share his
divine nature and escape the world's corruption caused by human desires.*
2 PETER 1:4 NLT

Today!

Lord, help me to rejoice in the time I have with my
family today. I don't want to dwell on what might
happen in the future; I want to relish this chance to
nurture and cherish the blessings You've given me.
Help me to live in the moment. Amen.

....
....
....
....
....
....
....
....
....
....
....
....
....
....
....
....
....
....

*"Therefore do not worry about tomorrow, for tomorrow will
worry about itself. Each day has enough trouble of its own."*
Matthew 6:34 niv

Teach Me to Discipline

Father, I want my children to know what I expect of them and then obey. Give me guidance to establish the right discipline system. I need strength in that area, Lord. I have started many times, but I get lazy and become inconsistent. I want to honor You by bringing up disciplined children. Amen.

No discipline seems pleasant at the time, but painful.
Later on, however, it produces a harvest of righteousness
and peace for those who have been trained by it.
HEBREWS 12:11 NIV

Patience by Example

God, You tell us in scripture that we should clothe ourselves
with patience. Still my complaining heart, O Lord. Fill me
with rejoicing. Help me to slow down and to take time for
others. I want to be an example of patience to those around
me. Give me strength for the task. Amen.

....

....

....

....

....

....

....

....

....

....

....

....

....

....

*Therefore, as God's chosen people, holy and dearly loved, clothe
yourselves with compassion, kindness, humility, gentleness and patience.*
COLOSSIANS 3:12 NIV

Song of Joy

Put a new song in my mouth, Lord. Let my children see
me being patient and waiting on You, no matter what
difficulty I'm facing. Help them learn the same song
of joy that You are giving me. Amen.

....
....
....
....
....
....
....
....
....
....
....
....
....
....
....
....
....

*There will be joy and songs of thanksgiving, and I will multiply my
people, not diminish them; I will honor them, not despise them.*
JEREMIAH 30:19 NLT

Faithfulness

Father, give me faithfulness in all things large and small,
so that I may be an example to my friends and family—
and to all those near me. Amen.

....
....
....
....
....
....
....
....
....
....
....
....
....
....

*She must be well respected by everyone because of the good she has
done. Has she brought up her children well? Has she been kind to
strangers and served other believers humbly? Has she helped those
who are in trouble? Has she always been ready to do good?*
1 Timothy 5:10 nlt

Fairness

Lord, help me not to judge, but to let You decide the
fairness of matters. Give me patience—to rest in You
and to wait for Your return. I need Your help to teach
my children to rest in You, too. Amen.

....
....
....
....
....
....
....
....
....
....
....
....
....
....

*Therefore judge nothing before the appointed time; wait until the
Lord comes. He will bring to light what is hidden in darkness
and will expose the motives of the heart. At that time each
will receive their praise from God.*
1 Corinthians 4:5 niv

Answered Prayer

Lord, when I see how You have interceded on my behalf,
I want to fall on my face before You. My prayers have been
answered in miraculous ways. In times when all I could see
was darkness, You provided light and power and hope. Amen.

....
....
....
....
....
....
....
....
....
....
....
....
....
....

*In the same way the Spirit also helps our weakness; for we do
not know how to pray as we should, but the Spirit Himself intercedes
for us with groanings too deep for words; and He who searches
the hearts knows what the mind of the Spirit is, because He
intercedes for the saints according to the will of God.*
ROMANS 8:26–27 NASB

Without Fear

Lord, the next time I am faced with danger for Your sake,
let me remember that You are faithful to reward Your
people, no matter how much I may fear. Amen.

....

....

....

....

....

....

....

....

....

....

....

....

....

....

....

*"And the one on whom seed was sown on the good soil, this is the man
who hears the word and understands it; who indeed bears fruit and
brings forth, some a hundredfold, some sixty, and some thirty."*
MATTHEW 13:23 NASB

Worthy

We give praise to many people and things that are unworthy, Father. Concert halls are sold out daily so that people may sing along with every word as an artist performs. We worship fashion, money, and social status. We give praise to mere men. Remind me when I begin to stray that You are the one true God and the only one who is worthy of praise. Amen.

I called to the Lord, who is worthy of praise,
and I have been saved from my enemies.
Psalm 18:3 niv

Small Beauty

Father, please don't let me fall into the trap of false pride.
Whatever small beauty I bring into this world is only a tiny
reflection of Your beauty, Your creation, Your perfection.
May I add a touch of beauty to Your world today through
a kind action or a generous deed. May my beauty always
come from within, where You abide in my heart. Amen.

*Charm is deceptive, and beauty is fleeting;
but a woman who fears the LORD is to be praised.*
PROVERBS 31:30 NIV

Comforting Opportunities

Set before me opportunities to comfort others as You comfort me. Help me to be ready to comfort a child or a friend in need, an aging parent, or even a complete stranger. We all need comfort at times. Amen.

Blessed be the God and Father of our Lord Jesus Christ, the Father of mercies and God of all comfort, who comforts us in all our affliction so that we will be able to comfort those who are in any affliction with the comfort with which we ourselves are comforted by God.
2 Corinthians 1:3–4 nasb

All I Need

Father, on days when I go off on my own, draw me close to You until I calm down and begin to think clearly. Everything is under control. All I need has been provided. Thank You. Amen.

....

....

....

....

....

....

....

....

....

....

....

....

....

....

....

....

And God is able to bless you abundantly, so that in all things at all times, having all that you need, you will abound in every good work.
2 Corinthians 9:8 niv

Loving Arms

Father, I can't begin to count the number of times You've wrapped Your loving arms around me and calmed me in the midst of fears. You've drawn me near in times of sorrow and given me assurance when I've faced great disappointment. I am thankful for the loving arms of my everlasting God. Amen.

The eternal God is a dwelling place,
and underneath are the everlasting arms.
DEUTERONOMY 33:27 NASB

Bring Joy

I am not always joyous, Father. At times I am downright
depressed. Please replace my sorrow with songs of joy.
I may have to sing for a while before the joy sinks in and
takes root. I love You, Father, and I want to learn to be
content and joyful in all circumstances. Amen.

Bring joy to your servant, Lord,
for I put my trust in you.
PSALM 86:4 NIV

Unconditional Love

Help me to love my friends and my family
with unconditional love. Amen.

....
....
....
....
....
....
....
....
....
....
....
....
....
....

*"So he returned home to his father. And while he was still a long
way off, his father saw him coming. Filled with love and compassion,
he ran to his son, embraced him, and kissed him. His son said to him,
'Father, I have sinned against both heaven and you, and I am no
longer worthy of being called your son.' But his father said to
the servants, 'Quick! Bring the finest robe in the house and put
it on him. Get a ring for his finger and sandals for his feet.'"*
LUKE 15:20–22 NLT

Learning to Obey

Father, I need to show the children in my life how important obedience is by being obedient myself—to You and to others in authority over me. Thank You for assisting me in this effort. Often, I want to go my own way. Show me that Your ways are always best. Bless me with a heart that obeys You quickly and without any hesitation. Amen.

Love the LORD your God and keep his requirements,
his decrees, his laws and his commands always.
DEUTERONOMY 11:1 NIV

I Lift Up My Soul

God, so many times I rush into my day headfirst
without stopping to spend time in prayer. Remind me
that I should lift up my day and my very soul to
You before I take one step. Amen.

*Let the morning bring me word of your unfailing love,
for I have put my trust in you. Show me the way
I should go, for to you I entrust my life.*
PSALM 143:8 NIV

A Woman of Value

Thank You for the work You have given me, Father,
with its opportunities to be of service to others and
to You. You have made me a woman of value,
and my contribution is great. Amen.

....

....

....

....

....

....

....

....

....

....

....

....

....

....

....

....

*"And the very hairs on your head are all numbered. So don't be afraid;
you are more valuable to God than a whole flock of sparrows."*
LUKE 12:7 NLT

A Living Sacrifice

Lord, make me a living sacrifice for You, that I might lead my family and others to You. Let my praises be a godly example in my home. I praise You with all that is within me. Amen.

....
....
....
....
....
....
....
....
....
....
....
....
....
....
....
....

And so, dear brothers and sisters, I plead with you to give your bodies to God because of all he has done for you. Let them be a living and holy sacrifice — the kind he will find acceptable. This is truly the way to worship him.
ROMANS 12:1 NLT

The Gift

Lord, one of the greatest gifts You've given me is
the Holy Spirit to intercede for me during prayer.
Thank You, Holy Spirit, for intervening and making
my requests better than I ever could. Amen.

_John answered their questions by saying, "I baptize you with water;
but someone is coming soon who is greater than I am—so much
greater that I'm not even worthy to be his slave and untie the straps of
his sandals. He will baptize you with the Holy Spirit and with fire."_
LUKE 3:16 NLT

With All My Heart

I want to follow You not with just part of me, but with all
of my heart. Hold me close, Father. Do what it takes in
my life to get me to the point of full surrender. I want to
mean it when I say that I surrender all. Amen.

....
....
....
....
....
....
....
....
....
....
....
....
....
....
....
....

*Teach me, LORD, the way of your decrees, that I may follow
it to the end. Give me understanding, so that I may
keep your law and obey it with all my heart.*
PSALM 119:33–34 NIV

A Merry Heart

Father, help me to get over self-doubt. Remind me that Your blessings are forever and I have nothing to fear. Give me a merry heart. Others will be drawn to me if I am joyful, but who wants to be around someone who is always complaining? Help me to be joyful so that others may know it is You who puts a smile on my face even in difficult times. Amen.

A cheerful heart is good medicine,
but a crushed spirit dries up the bones.
PROVERBS 17:22 NIV

Ruler of Oceans

No matter what happens to upset the surface, Father God,
You are in our innermost being, bringing peace and
comfort. Thank You that we can always trust You,
even in the midst of life's greatest storms. Amen.

You rule the oceans. You subdue their storm-tossed waves.
PSALM 89:9 NLT

To Be Humble

Father, help me to do my job humbly and to rely on You. That is what would please You most, and that reward is the best motivator I could ask for. Humble me that I might be lifted up. I ask this in the name of Jesus, who died for me. Amen.

Humble yourselves before the Lord,
and he will lift you up.
JAMES 4:10 NIV

The Mighty One

Father, as long as I trust in Your presence, I have nothing to worry about. Nothing can separate me from You, because You are the strong Protector, the mighty One who watches over me always. I praise You, Lord, for Your protection. Amen.

....
....
....
....
....
....
....
....
....
....
....
....
....
....
....

*But let all who take refuge in you be glad; let them
ever sing for joy. Spread your protection over them,
that those who love your name may rejoice in you.*
PSALM 5:11 NIV

Your Promises

Thank You, Lord, that Your Word is true. Help me to
look to Your steady and solid Word, not this world,
as my life instruction manual. I thank You that You
will never lead me astray, that You never lie to me,
and that You always keep Your promises. Amen.

....
....
....
....
....
....
....
....
....
....
....
....
....
....
....

Let us hold unswervingly to the hope we profess,
for he who promised is faithful.
HEBREWS 10:23 NIV

Control My Tongue, Lord

Lord, in the heat of anger, control my tongue, because
what I say then can be as damaging to my soul as it
is to my victim's reputation. Remove from me the
temptation to gossip, for no good comes from this.
Make me faithful in all things, Lord. Amen.

....
....
....
....
....
....
....
....
....
....
....
....
....
....
....

Women must likewise be dignified, not malicious
gossips, but temperate, faithful in all things.
1 TIMOTHY 3:11 NASB

Made Worthy

Lord, You stand before the throne of Your Father and
claim me as Your own, exempt from sin and judgment.
Because of Your sacrifice, I am made worthy. Because
You were presented as the spotless Lamb of God,
I am seen as righteous by my Father. He sees me
through a "Jesus lens." Thank You. Amen.

*When you have finished cleansing it, you shall present a young
bull without blemish and a ram without blemish from the flock.*
EZEKIEL 43:23 NASB

Reflections

Lord, help me realize that everything others say about me does not always reflect their true feelings. When others' words hurt me, show me how to explain this to them. I am "a good thing"—I deserve to be treated with respect. Amen.

....
....
....
....
....
....
....
....
....
....
....
....
....
....
....
....

The seeds of good deeds become a tree of life;
a wise person wins friends.
PROVERBS 11:30 NLT

To Be Pure

Lord, on days when I'm having spiritual struggles,
my thoughts become full of discouragement and frustration.
I don't like to be so controlled by my emotions. Please give
me the strength to be pure in every situation. Amen.

....
....
....
....
....
....
....
....
....
....
....
....
....
....
....

*Finally, brothers and sisters, whatever is true, whatever is noble, whatever
is right, whatever is pure, whatever is lovely, whatever is admirable —
if anything is excellent or praiseworthy —think about such things.*
PHILIPPIANS 4:8 NIV

Heart Friends

Lord, You know how painful it is when things are not right
between friends. What a joy it is to know that I am made
right with You by faith. We can communicate freely,
talking and listening, enjoying each other as heart friends.
Thank You for restoration and righteousness. Amen.

*Since, then, you have been raised with Christ, set your hearts on
things above, where Christ is, seated at the right hand of God.*
COLOSSIANS 3:1 NIV

Surrounded by Love

Lord, Your promise of protection gives me a secure feeling.
I'm surrounded by Your love and protection. Because
You love me and care for me, I can do the same for others.
Thank You for the peace this brings. Amen.

_But I am like an olive tree flourishing in the house of God;
I trust in God's unfailing love for ever and ever._
PSALM 52:8 NIV

Redefining Greatness

Lord, help me to redefine *greatness* for others and show them worthy examples of those who have received You. They need to know that there is a better, more glorious way to live. Amen.

....
....
....
....
....
....
....
....
....
....
....
....
....
....
....
....

Now faith is confidence in what we hope for and assurance about what we do not see. This is what the ancients were commended for. By faith we understand that the universe was formed at God's command, so that what is seen was not made out of what was visible.
HEBREWS 11:1–3 NIV

Obedience

Lord, I want to obey You in everything and also lead the children in my life to obey You. Through our obedience to You, help us to reach many people for Your Kingdom. Amen.

....
....
....
....
....
....
....
....
....
....
....
....
....
....
....
....

"Whether it is favorable or unfavorable, we will obey the Lord our God, to whom we are sending you, so that it will go well with us, for we will obey the Lord our God."
JEREMIAH 42:6 NIV

Victory

Lord, show me the path to victory every day, because sometimes I find it hard to follow. You know every turn in the road, and I will follow You in security all the days of my life. Make my paths straight as I acknowledge You as Lord of my life. I ask these things humbly in the name of Your Son, Jesus. Amen.

....

....

....

....

....

....

....

....

....

....

....

....

....

....

....

....

In all your ways acknowledge Him,
and He will make your paths straight.
PROVERBS 3:6 NASB

Pleasures

Lord, thank You for Your gift of physical pleasures, but teach us to use them wisely, according to Your wishes for us. Keep us faithful to our spouses and to Your laws of self-control. Help us not even to entertain the idea of adultery. Amen.

"You have heard that it was said, 'You shall not commit adultery.'
But I tell you that anyone who looks at a woman lustfully has
already committed adultery with her in his heart."
MATTHEW 5:27–28 NIV

Grief

When grief comes to me, Father, I know You understand my suffering and long to comfort me. I am thankful that I do not grieve as those who have no hope. My loved ones who had accepted You are in a glorious place now! Give me a drive and a determination to pray for my lost loved ones. I do not want any of them to miss out on eternal life with You. Amen.

....
....
....
....
....
....
....
....
....
....
....
....
....

Brothers and sisters, we do not want you to be uninformed about those who sleep in death, so that you do not grieve like the rest of mankind, who have no hope.
1 THESSALONIANS 4:13 NIV

The Fruits of My Labor

When I grow old, Lord, I pray that I will see the fruits
of my labor and rejoice, knowing that all my efforts
were well worth the time and energy I put into them.
Help me not to dread old age but help me also never
to waste a day I have been given. Amen.

*A gray head is a crown of glory;
it is found in the way of righteousness.*
PROVERBS 16:31 NASB

All Day Long

God, my hope is in You from the moment I wake up
in the morning until I lay my head down on my pillow
at night. Please give me the ability to find hope even
in situations that may seem hopeless. Amen.

*Show me your ways, LORD, teach me your paths.
Guide me in your truth and teach me, for you are
God my Savior, and my hope is in you all day long.*
PSALM 25:4–5 NIV

My Hope

Lord, You are my hope in an often hopeless world. You are my hope of heaven, my hope of peace, my hope of change, purpose, and unconditional love. Fill the reservoir of my heart to overflowing with the joy that real hope brings. Amen.

....

....

....

....

....

....

....

....

....

....

....

....

....

....

....

....

....

*For in hope we have been saved, but hope that is seen
is not hope; for who hopes for what he already sees?*
ROMANS 8:24 NASB

Assurance

Lord, help me to put aside my needs, to draw others close,
and to assure them of my love and, more importantly,
of Your love. Faith in You brings an assurance like
no other available to men. Amen.

....

....

....

....

....

....

....

....

....

....

....

....

....

....

....

*Let us draw near to God with a sincere heart and with the full
assurance that faith brings, having our hearts sprinkled to cleanse us
from a guilty conscience and having our bodies washed with pure water.*
HEBREWS 10:22 NIV

True Love

Thank You, Jesus, for Your sacrificial love for me.
Thank You for the example of true love that You have
provided. May I be crucified with You and allow You
to reign in my heart and live through me. Amen.

....
....
....
....
....
....
....
....
....
....
....
....
....
....
....

*I have been crucified with Christ; and it is no longer I who live, but
Christ lives in me; and the life which I now live in the flesh I live by
faith in the Son of God, who loved me and gave Himself up for me.*
GALATIANS 2:20 NASB

Eternal Promise

Thank You for Your promise to preserve me if I love
You, Father. I know that this is an eternal promise.
What more incentive do I need to pursue a right walk
with You? Keep me on the right path, Lord. Amen.

O love the LORD, all you His godly ones! The LORD
preserves the faithful and fully recompenses the proud doer.
PSALM 31:23 NASB

Count It All Joy

Lord, You are made strong in my weaknesses. I need Your help to remember that and to teach the children in my life that we should count it all joy when we are faced with trials and suffering. We await a wonderful eternity in heaven with You, where all of this earthly "stuff" will fade away. The things of God are all that really matter. Amen.

You suffered along with those in prison and joyfully accepted the confiscation of your property, because you knew that you yourselves had better and lasting possessions.
HEBREWS 10:34 NIV

Our Protector

Hear the cries of Your people, Father. Just as You did in ancient times, I pray that You will protect and deliver us. In the name of Jesus I pray, amen.

....
....
....
....
....
....
....
....
....
....
....
....
....
....
....
....

The LORD is king forever and ever! The godless nations will vanish from the land. LORD, you know the hopes of the helpless. Surely you will hear their cries and comfort them. You will bring justice to the orphans and the oppressed, so mere people can no longer terrify them.
PSALM 10:16–18 NLT

Completion of God's Plan

Lord, help me realize that my understanding is not necessary for the completion of Your plan. You understand everything; all I need to do is have faith. You will complete the good work You have begun in my life. Please use me in any way You so desire. Amen.

....

....

....

....

....

....

....

....

....

....

....

....

....

....

Being confident of this, that he who began a good work in you will carry it on to completion until the day of Christ Jesus.
PHILIPPIANS 1:6 NIV

The Lord Is with You!

God, You have been with Your children throughout the ages.
Nothing has changed. You are the same yesterday, today,
and tomorrow. Remind me of Your steadfast love and make
me courageous enough to speak Your name and witness to
others about salvation in Jesus. Amen.

*"Stand still and watch the LORD's victory. He is with you,
O people of Judah and Jerusalem. Do not be afraid or discouraged.
Go out against them tomorrow, for the LORD is with you!"*
2 CHRONICLES 20:17 NLT

Cleansed by the Blood

I've made mistakes, Lord. But someday You will present me faultless, cleansed by Your blood. The evidence of Your power to lift me up and make me whole fills me with exceeding joy. I will praise You forever and forever. Amen.

....

....

....

....

....

....

....

....

....

....

....

....

....

The more you grow like this, the more productive and useful you will be in your knowledge of our Lord Jesus Christ. But those who fail to develop in this way are shortsighted or blind, forgetting that they have been cleansed from their old sins.
2 PETER 1:8–9 NLT

Inner Strength

Lord, I can see Your inner power at work in my children as they grow in You. Your Spirit inside us is a life-changing power that will always be available to us wherever we are. Thank You for this wonderful gift. Amen.

David was greatly distressed because the men were talking of stoning him; each one was bitter in spirit because of his sons and daughters. But David found strength in the LORD his God.
1 SAMUEL 30:6 NIV

A Close Walk

Father God, joy fills my life when a child asks me to
read a book to him and then he chooses one about You.
I pray that this is the beginning of a close walk that
he will eventually have with You. Amen.

*Start children off on the way they should go,
and even when they are old they will not turn from it.*
PROVERBS 22:6 NIV

Steadfast and Dedicated

Father, my daily problems come and go; yet if I remain
steadfast and dedicated, doing the work You have
given me to do, I am confident that my reward awaits
me in heaven. Give me the endurance that I need to
press on in the faith. Thank You, Lord. Amen.

*"Rejoice and be glad, because great is your reward in heaven,
for in the same way they persecuted the prophets who were before you."*
MATTHEW 5:12 NIV

Priorities

Father, praising You and rejoicing in You must
be high on my priority list. Proclaiming Your
love to others must never be lacking in my life.
Thank You that I am able to rejoice in You! Amen.

....
....
....
....
....
....
....
....
....
....
....
....
....
....
....

*Jesus replied: "Love the Lord your God with all your
heart and with all your soul and with all your mind."*
MATTHEW 22:37 NIV

Reflecting Glory

Gracious Father, I thank You for the work I have. You made work, and it is part of every man and woman's life. May I do my work, whether in the home or beyond its walls, in a way that is pleasing to You and that reflects Your glory. Amen.

The Lord God took the man and put him in the Garden of Eden to work it and take care of it.
Genesis 2:15 niv

Be Joyful

There's no mistaking, Lord. You've made it clear that
I'm to be joyful in each and every task. The next time
I'm tempted to complain about the mounds of work,
remind me to turn my murmuring into praise. Amen.

*Though the fig tree does not bud and there are no grapes on the
vines, though the olive crop fails and the fields produce no food,
though there are no sheep in the pen and no cattle in the stalls,
yet I will rejoice in the LORD, I will be joyful in God my Savior.*
HABAKKUK 3:17–18 NIV

The Good Shepherd

Father, Your guidance is trustworthy. You are our Good
Shepherd. You lead us to places of rest when we need them.
I need that rest. Thank You for Your leading. Amen.

*Then, because so many people were coming and going that they
did not even have a chance to eat, he said to them, "Come with
me by yourselves to a quiet place and get some rest."*
MARK 6:31 NIV

Not Shaken

I am not like those who do not know You, Lord.
Disaster shakes them. Even if I walk through the
valley of the shadow of death, I will not be shaken.
My God goes with me. You are my hope, and I
find my rest and calm assurance in You. Amen.

*Yes, my soul, find rest in God; my hope comes from him. Truly he is
my rock and my salvation; he is my fortress, I will not be shaken.*
PSALM 62:5–6 NIV

The Right Example

Lord, when I am old, I want my children to respect and love me. By my actions toward others, I am always teaching— either respect or disrespect. I want to set the right example for my children as I honor older people. Amen.

....

....

....

....

....

....

....

....

....

....

....

....

....

....

....

....

*"Stand up in the presence of the aged, show respect
for the elderly and revere your God. I am the Lord."*
LEVITICUS 19:32 NIV

Humble Me

Humble me, Lord. Fill me with the desire to hearken to my parents. I can learn so much from them and benefit from their life experiences. I believe this is Your will. Thank You for Your patience and guidance. Amen.

....
....
....
....
....
....
....
....
....
....
....
....
....
....

"Honor your father and your mother, as the LORD your God has commanded you, so that you may live long and that it may go well with you in the land the LORD your God is giving you."
DEUTERONOMY 5:16 NIV

Great Expectations

Lord, You've given me a life that abounds with
rich blessings; You've guaranteed that because
of this, You also have great expectations of me.
Help me to be faithful to these expectations. Amen.

....
....
....
....
....
....
....
....
....
....
....
....
....
....

"But the one who does not know and does things deserving
punishment will be beaten with few blows. From everyone who
has been given much, much will be demanded; and from the one
who has been entrusted with much, much more will be asked."
LUKE 12:48 NIV

On Level Ground

God, the society in which I live is shaky. It is unsteady and unstable. The fashions and priorities shift with the days. I want to build my house upon the stability of Your Word. I want to do Your will even in a world that says it is fine to do as I feel. Please lead me on level ground. Make my way straight before me and teach me to look neither left, nor right, but to follow hard after my God. Amen.

....

....

....

....

....

....

....

....

....

....

....

....

....

Teach me to do your will, for you are my God;
may your good Spirit lead me on level ground.
PSALM 143:10 NIV

Taking Up My Cross

Lord, here I am before You. I am ready to "take up my cross" and follow You. Every day I want to be with You, empowered by You, and loved so deeply that I am changed. Show me what it means to lose my life in order to save it. Amen.

And He was saying to them all, "If anyone wishes to come after Me, he must deny himself, and take up his cross daily and follow Me."
LUKE 9:23 NASB

Godly Responses

Lord, what a blessing it is that You have given us such an array of emotions with which to express ourselves. Help me to be more like You—slow to anger and abounding in love. Help me to be a woman who is forgiving. Amen.

....
....
....
....
....
....
....
....
....
....
....
....
....
....
....

*"But You are a God of forgiveness, gracious and compassionate,
slow to anger and abounding in lovingkindness;
and You did not forsake them."*
NEHEMIAH 9:17 NASB

Growing Spiritually

Lord, I want to grow up spiritually. I want to move from head knowledge to heart experience with You. I want to know what it means to enjoy Your presence, not just to make requests. Step by step and day by day, teach me to follow and learn Your ways. Amen.

When I was a child, I used to speak like a child,
think like a child, reason like a child; when I
became a man, I did away with childish things.
1 CORINTHIANS 13:11 NASB

For Your Mercy

Thank You, Jesus, for calling sinners to repentance. If You had come only for the righteous, I would not have been called, for I am a sinner. I thank You for Your mercy. Amen.

....

....

....

....

....

....

....

....

....

....

....

....

....

....

....

*Then it happened that as Jesus was reclining at the table
in the house, behold, many tax collectors and sinners
came and were dining with Jesus and His disciples.*
MATTHEW 9:10 NASB

The Humble Spirit

Heavenly Father, we live in a world that lifts up
proud people. Make us all aware of how much
You value sacrifice. Help us to have the humble
spirit we need when we come before You. Amen.

*He has told you, O man, what is good; and what does the
LORD require of you but to do justice, to love kindness,
and to walk humbly with your God?*
MICAH 6:8 NASB

Whole

Father, the life I am living right now is not the result of my faith in You but of Your faith in me. Thank You for Your sacrifice, which saves me and makes me whole. Amen.

Consider it all joy, my brethren, when you encounter various trials, knowing that the testing of your faith produces endurance. And let endurance have its perfect result, so that you may be perfect and complete, lacking in nothing.
JAMES 1:2–4 NASB

Everywhere

Lord, there is so much I do not understand about You.
Still, I can see the effects of Your actions, the evidence that
You are still active in my daily life. I do not need to physically
see You to believe. Your evidence is everywhere. Amen.

....
....
....
....
....
....
....
....
....
....
....
....
....
....
....
....

For since the creation of the world His invisible attributes, His eternal
power and divine nature, have been clearly seen, being understood
through what has been made, so that they are without excuse.
ROMANS 1:20 NASB

Example of Compassion

Lord, help me to show compassion for children and also for strangers. You were the best example. You loved everyone, Lord. You gave Your life for all people. Help me do the same, and in doing so set an example for others. Amen.

But the angel said to them, "Do not be afraid. I bring you good news that will cause great joy for all the people."
LUKE 2:10 NIV

No More Hiding

Lord, I can no longer hide in the darkness of my guilt
and sin. You already know everything I've done wrong,
yet You bring me into the light—not to condemn,
nor to condone, but to heal me. I acknowledge my
wrongs and confess them all to You, Lord. Amen.

....

....

....

....

....

....

....

....

....

....

....

....

....

....

*Woe to those who go to great depths to hide their plans
from the LORD, who do their work in darkness
and think, "Who sees us? Who will know?"*
ISAIAH 29:15 NIV

Victory over Death

Lord, thank You for Your gift of eternal life and the power to do Your will. I cannot fathom how You suffered, yet You did it all for me—for every person. You bled for my sins. You had victory over death. You made a way for me. Thank You, Lord. Amen.

....

....

....

....

....

....

....

....

....

....

....

....

....

....

....

....

....

The sting of death is sin, and the power of sin is the law. But thanks be to God! He gives us the victory through our Lord Jesus Christ.
1 Corinthians 15:56–57 niv

Heart of Compassion

Lord, Your compassion for people is great. Create in me a
heart of compassion—enlarge my vision so I see and help
the poor, the sick, the people who don't know You, and the
people whose concerns You lay upon my heart. Just as You
are gracious and compassionate, teach me to overflow with
grace and mercy to those around me, I pray. Amen.

The LORD is gracious and righteous;
our God is full of compassion.
PSALM 116:5 NIV

Help Me to Wait

Father, when my children do wrong, I want them to admit
it and ask for forgiveness. From Your example with me,
I know there are times when I need to wait for my children's
repentance. Help me to wait, Lord. Amen.

*Whoever is patient has great understanding,
but one who is quick-tempered displays folly.*
PROVERBS 14:29 NIV

A New Creation in Christ

Lord, now that I am devoted to You heart and soul,
I am a new creation. Thank You for washing away my
old ways of thinking and behaving, and for empowering
me to live a new life. Your love changes me! Amen.

*Therefore, if anyone is in Christ, the new creation
has come: The old has gone, the new is here!*
2 CORINTHIANS 5:17 NIV

Patient Endurance

Thank You, Lord. You have given me a wonderful example of patient endurance. When I am losing my patience, I recall how long You waited for me to repent and turn to You. Amen.

The Lord is not slow about His promise, as some count slowness, but is patient toward you, not wishing for any to perish but for all to come to repentance.
2 PETER 3:9 NASB

What a Blessing!

Thank You, Lord, for putting other godly women in my
life. They face many temptations and struggles that I
face, but they've committed themselves to purity and
godliness, so together we can encourage one another.
What a blessing it is to have a circle of Christian friends!
Help me never to take them for granted and remind
me to lift them up in prayer regularly. Amen.

*A friend loves at all times,
and a brother is born for adversity.*
PROVERBS 17:17 NASB

My Prayer Life

Lord, I long to be more connected to You. Teach me
to worship You as the true Source of power and love.
I adore You like no other. Transform me so my prayers
will be powerful and my life will be fruitful. Amen.

....
....
....
....
....
....
....
....
....
....
....
....
....
....
....

*Therefore, confess your sins to one another, and pray for
one another so that you may be healed. The effective
prayer of a righteous man can accomplish much.*
JAMES 5:16 NASB

Blameless

God, sometimes I slip up or make a mistake. I sin without
meaning to do so. Other times, I am tempted and I follow
Satan's detour willingly. I move away from You and I seek
things that are unhealthy and not godly. This can bring great
destruction to my life. I have seen it in others' lives as they
have crumbled away. I don't want this for my life. Make me
blameless before You. Keep me from willful sin, I pray. Amen.

*Keep your servant also from willful sins; may they not rule over me.
Then I will be blameless, innocent of great transgression.*
PSALM 19:13 NIV

A Friend

Lord, sometimes I need another person to talk to who understands what I'm going through. Help me find a friend—someone who needs the kind of companionship I do. I need a friend, and I would like to be a good friend to another as well. Amen.

....
....
....
....
....
....
....
....
....
....
....
....
....
....

*A friend loves at all times, and a
brother is born for a time of adversity.*
PROVERBS 17:17 NIV

Listen Up

Father, I get discouraged when I don't know which way
to go. Remind me that You are right behind me, telling me
which way to turn. Help me to be quiet and listen for Your
guidance. Sometimes it comes through Your still, small voice.
I cannot hear Your instruction or heed Your directions
if I am not focused and listening. Amen.

*Good and upright is the LORD; therefore
he instructs sinners in his ways.*
PSALM 25:8 NIV

How to Trust

Lord, I'm ashamed to admit that sometimes I have a hard time taking You at Your Word. Please show me how to trust You more, even when my mind can't grasp it and my heart can't accept it. Help me never to trust more in man or in man-made things than I trust in my heavenly Father. Amen.

"Do not put your trust in idols or make metal images of gods for yourselves. I am the LORD your God."
LEVITICUS 19:4 NLT

Joy and Strength

Thank You, God, for Your Word. It instructs me on how to
live. It brings joy to my days and gives me strength when
I am weak. You are my joy. You are my strength. Amen.

....
....
....
....
....
....
....
....
....
....
....
....
....
....
....
....

*The LORD is my strength and shield. I trust him with
all my heart. He helps me, and my heart is filled
with joy. I burst out in songs of thanksgiving.*
PSALM 28:7 NLT

Into Glory

Thank You, Father, for the calm assurance that one
day I will be with You in heaven. Jesus is preparing
a place for me there even now. I am doubly blessed
because I have been given this abundant life on earth
and eternal life with You in glory. Amen.

You guide me with your counsel,
and afterward you will take me into glory.
PSALM 73:24 NIV

The Best

Lord, I need Your gentle wisdom for every area of life.
I'm so thankful that what You offer is the best. Amen.

....

....

....

....

....

....

....

....

....

....

....

....

....

....

....

*"You fathers—if your children ask for a fish, do you give them
a snake instead? Or if they ask for an egg, do you give them a
scorpion? Of course not! So if you sinful people know how to give
good gifts to your children, how much more will your heavenly
Father give the Holy Spirit to those who ask him."*
LUKE 11:11–13 NLT

Give and It Will Be Given unto You

Lord, You told me to give and that if I do, it shall be given to me. Your generosity is unmatched, and Your blessings are always wonderful. Thank You! Amen.

....

....

....

....

....

....

....

....

....

....

....

....

....

"Give, and it will be given to you. A good measure, pressed down, shaken together and running over, will be poured into your lap. For with the measure you use, it will be measured to you."

LUKE 6:38 NIV

Slowing Down

Father, I need rest—rest from my schedule, rest from the demands of my family, rest from "doing" to a place of simply "being." Lead me to that place. Calm my mind and my emotions so I can slow down enough to find real rest. Amen.

....
....
....
....
....
....
....
....
....
....
....
....
....
....
....
....

"Take my yoke upon you and learn from me, for I am gentle and humble in heart, and you will find rest for your souls. For my yoke is easy and my burden is light."
MATTHEW 11:29–30 NIV

Make Me an Instrument

Lord, I want to be instrumental in helping my family
establish a close walk with You. Direct me daily to
renew my commitment to follow in Your steps.
Thank You for being the example I need. Amen.

*Let us therefore make every effort to do what
leads to peace and to mutual edification.*
ROMANS 14:19 NIV

I Will Fear No Evil

I have no reason to fear, God. I may walk through some tough times. Eventually, I will face the valley of the shadow of death. But I will not face it alone. You are always with me, protecting me and guiding me. You are my comfort and my shield. I am so thankful that You are my Good Shepherd. Amen.

....
....
....
....
....
....
....
....
....
....
....
....
....
....
....
....

Even though I walk through the darkest valley, I will fear no evil,
for you are with me; your rod and your staff, they comfort me.
PSALM 23:4 NIV

No Matter What

Lord, remove the fears that bind me so that I can be
happy in the knowledge that You are there to comfort
me—no matter what else is happening. Amen.

....

....

....

....

....

....

....

....

....

....

....

....

....

....

*Not that I was ever in need, for I have learned how to be content
with whatever I have. I know how to live on almost nothing or with
everything. I have learned the secret of living in every situation,
whether it is with a full stomach or empty, with plenty or little.*
PHILIPPIANS 4:11–12 NLT

Teach Me to Relax

Heavenly Father, I find it hard to find time to relax.
Thank You for making me to lie down even when
I don't want to. Thank You for leading me beside
quiet waters when I need the solace. Amen.

....
....
....
....
....
....
....
....
....
....
....
....
....
....
....
....

The LORD is my shepherd; I have all that I need.
He lets me rest in green meadows; he leads me beside
peaceful streams. He renews my strength.
PSALM 23:1–3 NLT

Heart Cleansing

Lord, let me know when I am wrong. That way I
can come to You for cleansing and an opportunity
to make things right. Thank You for the truth in
Your Word, even though sometimes the truth hurts.
Help me to grow as a result of correction, I pray. Amen.

*If you reject discipline, you only harm yourself;
but if you listen to correction, you grow in understanding.*
PROVERBS 15:32 NLT

A Constant Reminder

As I read Your Word, it is a constant reminder of Your love for me. It also reminds me of how much You love my family and that You have their best interests at heart, too. Amen.

....

....

....

....

....

....

....

....

....

....

....

....

....

....

....

And hope does not put us to shame, because God's love has been poured out into our hearts through the Holy Spirit, who has been given to us.
ROMANS 5:5 NIV

Before Me

I pray that You will go before me, God. I cannot see
more than one step at a time, but You see the path that
You have set me on. You see the future, and You know
the ways in which I should go. Go before me, walk beside
me, and stay near to me, I pray. I believe that I can do
all things because You are with me. Amen.

I keep my eyes always on the LORD.
With him at my right hand, I will not be shaken.
PSALM 16:8 NIV

Help Me to Live by Your Word

Lord, help me study Your Word and grow in knowledge
of You in order to attain godliness. Then I can help
others around me to understand how to live godly lives.
Help me to place a high priority on reading and
applying Your holy Word. Amen.

*All Scripture is God-breathed and is useful for teaching,
rebuking, correcting and training in righteousness.*
2 TIMOTHY 3:16 NIV

Attitude Adjustment

Lord, I need an attitude adjustment that can only come from
You. Let me be a cheerful worker. Resolve my conflicted
feelings and give me Your peace. Amen.

....

....

....

....

....

....

....

....

....

....

....

....

....

*Create in me a pure heart, O God, and renew a steadfast spirit
within me. Do not cast me from your presence or take your
Holy Spirit from me. Restore to me the joy of your salvation
and grant me a willing spirit, to sustain me.*
PSALM 51:10–12 NIV

Faithful Companion

Be with all women living alone, Lord. Be especially near
to their hearts, I pray. Whether they are single, divorced,
or widowed, be their faithful Companion and Guide as they
strive to build a life based on Your principles. Amen.

*For your Maker is your husband — the LORD Almighty
is his name — the Holy One of Israel is your Redeemer;
he is called the God of all the earth.*

ISAIAH 54:5 NIV

Give Love

Lord, help me not to be quick to judge or oppose love between others. Let me give love time to do its work. I may never see the result I want, but I am sure it is in Your hands. Amen.

....
....
....
....
....
....
....
....
....
....
....
....
....

Love is patient, love is kind. It does not envy, it does not boast, it is not proud. It does not dishonor others, it is not self-seeking, it is not easily angered, it keeps no record of wrongs. Love does not delight in evil but rejoices with the truth. It always protects, always trusts, always hopes, always perseveres. Love never fails.

1 CORINTHIANS 13:4–8 NIV

Have Mercy on Me

Merciful God, You have forgiven me in the past and
I ask You to show mercy yet again. You are a gracious
God, and I am so thankful for Your open arms and
for second chances. I love You, Lord. Amen.

*Have mercy on me, my God, have mercy on me, for in you
I take refuge. I will take refuge in the shadow of your wings.*
PSALM 57:1 NIV

Thank You!

Father, thank You for all You have given me, for all You have taught me, and for all the good times still to come. I do not have to worry about the future because I am Your daughter and You have good plans for me. You have promised never to leave me or forsake me. Thank You for Your promises, Lord. They bring such peace to my life. Amen.

....

....

....

....

....

....

....

....

....

....

....

....

....

....

She is clothed with strength and dignity;
she can laugh at the days to come.
PROVERBS 31:25 NIV

Fill Me with Faith

I often feel that I lack faith, Lord, that You must be speaking
promises for someone else — someone more faithful and
deserving of them. Show me the error of this thinking. Amen.

....
....
....
....
....
....
....
....
....
....
....
....
....
....
....
....

*He replied, "Because you have so little faith. Truly I tell you,
if you have faith as small as a mustard seed, you can say
to this mountain, 'Move from here to there,' and it
will move. Nothing will be impossible for you."*
MATTHEW 17:20 NIV

My Fortress

Dear Heavenly Father, You are a mighty tower, my fortress, a refuge I can always run to. You protect Your own. In times of trouble, I am comforted to know that You are always on my side. Thank You for this assurance, mighty God. Amen.

You are my strength, I watch for you; you, God, are my fortress, my God on whom I can rely.
PSALM 59:9–10 NIV

Keep Me from Temptation

Lord, I am human and often tempted. I want to honor You
with my life, and yet I find myself straying. Be with me when
I am tempted and show me the true joys of self-control.
Make me a daughter who represents her heavenly Father
well in the world. I ask these things in Jesus' name, amen.

*No temptation has overtaken you except what is common to
mankind. And God is faithful; he will not let you be tempted
beyond what you can bear. But when you are tempted,
he will also provide a way out so that you can endure it.*
1 Corinthians 10:13 NIV

My Rock

Lord, You alone are my rock. You are my fortress. You deliver me from evil, and whenever there is trouble in my life, I take refuge in You. You are my shield, my salvation, and my stronghold (Psalm 18:2). You are all I need. Amen.

Turn your ear to me, come quickly to my rescue;
be my rock of refuge, a strong fortress to save me.
PSALM 31:2 NIV

The Peacekeeper

Lord, help me be the peacekeeper, never the one who stirs
up more anger. Help me be an example to my whole family
and to my friends and coworkers. You offer peace to me that
the world cannot give. Help others to see that peace in me
and long for it themselves, I pray. May others come to
know You by seeing Jesus in me. Amen.

Great peace have those who love your law,
and nothing can make them stumble.
PSALM 119:165 NIV

Never Alone

Father, when troubles come, I never have to face them alone. Thank You for always being with me as my refuge and strength. When all else fails, I put my trust in You and am never disappointed. You have promised me in Your Word that nothing can separate me from You. Amen.

....

....

....

....

....

....

....

....

....

....

....

....

....

....

My Father, who has given them to me, is greater than all;
no one can snatch them out of my Father's hand.
JOHN 10:29 NIV

The Victor

Precious Father, on my own, I am bound to fail. Now that I have put my trust in You, I cannot fail, for You are always the Victor, and this knowledge makes me strong where once I was weak. Amen.

....

....

....

....

....

....

....

....

....

....

....

....

....

....

....

"The LORD your God is with you, the Mighty Warrior who saves. He will take great delight in you; in his love he will no longer rebuke you, but will rejoice over you with singing."
ZEPHANIAH 3:17 NIV

A Virtuous Woman

Lord, I want to help bring others to You, to be judged
a virtuous woman for Your sake, not for any glory that
might come to me. Use me as You see fit, because any
work You give me to do is an honor. Amen.

....
....
....
....
....
....
....
....
....
....
....
....
....
....
....
....
....

Who can find a virtuous and capable wife? She is more precious than
rubies. Her husband can trust her, and she will greatly enrich his life.
She brings him good, not harm, all the days of her life.
PROVERBS 31:10–12 NLT

My Time

Help me invest my time in more worthy pursuits, Lord,
ones that will provide lasting satisfaction. I'm not sure what
You will ask of me, but I am willing to try anything You
recommend and give any resulting praise to You. Amen.

....

....

....

....

....

....

....

....

....

....

....

....

....

....

*Work willingly at whatever you do, as though you were
working for the Lord rather than for people. Remember
that the Lord will give you an inheritance as your reward,
and that the Master you are serving is Christ.*
COLOSSIANS 3:23–24 NLT

Do Not Be Afraid

Mighty God, I do not have to fight the battle that is before me. I must simply take my position and trust in You to deliver me. This is not my battle but Yours. I will not be afraid or discouraged. I will face this fight, and You will be with me (2 Chronicles 20:17). Amen.

"Do not be afraid! Don't be discouraged by this mighty army, for the battle is not yours, but God's."
2 CHRONICLES 20:15 NLT

Much-Needed Courage

Father, I need the courage of a soldier going into battle.
Each day I am on the front lines of a spiritual battle.
Satan would love to see me fail. Help me. Go before me
into battle. Give me supernatural courage that can
only come from You. Amen.

*"So be strong and courageous! Do not be afraid and do not
panic before them. For the LORD your God will personally
go ahead of you. He will neither fail you nor abandon you."*
DEUTERONOMY 31:6 NLT

Grant Me Strength

Lord, I would prefer to live a life of peace, but when I must fight for those I love, I pray You will give me the strength to do so. When I must stand up for what is right, I pray for the right words and actions. Amen.

_____

_____

_____

_____

_____

_____

_____

_____

_____

_____

_____

_____

_____

_____

_____

That is why, for Christ's sake, I delight in weaknesses,
in insults, in hardships, in persecutions, in difficulties.
For when I am weak, then I am strong.
2 Corinthians 12:10 niv

Consolation and Comfort

There are wars and rumors of wars, Father. I ask for Your comfort for all the wives and mothers who sit and wait, regardless of where their loved ones are serving in the military forces. Thank You for Your consolation and comfort. Amen.

"Peace I leave with you; my peace I give you. I do not give to you as the world gives. Do not let your hearts be troubled and do not be afraid."
JOHN 14:27 NIV

Just Right

Thank You, Lord, for being so faithful. Thank You for Your compassion—which is just the right amount to get me through the day. Give me each day my daily bread, I pray. Amen.

....

....

....

....

....

....

....

....

....

....

....

....

....

....

....

Keep falsehood and lies far from me; give me neither poverty nor riches, but give me only my daily bread.
PROVERBS 30:8 NIV

The Shepherd

Dear Jesus, You are my Good Shepherd. You have sacrificed Your very life for me. I know Your voice (John 10:4). I will follow it all the days of my life. If I go astray and listen to another voice, I pray that You will lead me back to the right path. I love You, Savior. Amen.

....
....
....
....
....
....
....
....
....
....
....
....
....
....

Save your people and bless your inheritance;
be their shepherd and carry them forever.
PSALM 28:9 NIV

Godly Woman

Lord, help me to be a godly woman. May others notice my
loving spirit rather than the name brands that I wear.
May my beauty come from within. May friends and even
acquaintances be blessed for time spent in my presence.
May my deeds reflect the great love and grace that You
have shown me. In Jesus' name I pray, amen.

....

....

....

....

....

....

....

....

....

....

....

I also want the women to dress modestly, with decency and
propriety, adorning themselves, not with elaborate hairstyles
or gold or pearls or expensive clothes, but with good deeds,
appropriate for women who profess to worship God.
1 Timothy 2:9–11 niv

The Answers

Father, I know my understanding is weak. But when I am in need of guidance, the first place I turn to is Your Word. Help me to search diligently, for I know the answers I need are there. May Your Word be hidden in my heart so that I may not sin against You (Psalm 119:11). Amen.

Jesus answered, "It is written: 'Man shall not live on bread alone, but on every word that comes from the mouth of God.'"
MATTHEW 4:4 NIV

Let the Light Shine

Lord, if there's one thing I need, it is trustworthy guidance.
In darkness or light, on fair days or foul, I trust that the light of
Your Word will bring me safely home. I am so thankful that I
can trust in the darkness what I have seen in the light. Amen.

The light shines in the darkness,
and the darkness can never extinguish it.
JOHN 1:5 NLT

Advice

Lord, show me my errors and teach me the proper way to take advice. Help me always to seek godly counsel. I can be so stubborn, but I know that I need to receive advice at times in order to make good decisions. Grant me a more open mind and heart. Put in my path women to mentor me, women who have attained godly wisdom over the years. Such women are rare treasures. Amen.

The wise in heart are called discerning,
and gracious words promote instruction.
PROVERBS 16:21 NIV

For Good

Father, give me Your peace and an understanding
that all things work together for good when
I follow Your will. Amen.

*Commit to the LORD whatever you do, and he will establish
your plans. The LORD works out everything to its proper end.*
PROVERBS 16:3–4 NIV

Right Paths

Father, Your Word contains the best instruction and advice
I could ever possess. Give me the wisdom to weigh
everything else I read against what the Bible says.
Thank You for leading me in right paths. Amen.

_He refreshes my soul. He guides me
along the right paths for his name's sake._
PSALM 23:3 NIV

Called to Be Godly

Lord, I'm called to live a godly life—not by
childishness, but by Your grace and virtue.
Thank You for Your provision. Amen.

*Finally, all of you, be like-minded, be sympathetic, love one another,
be compassionate and humble. Do not repay evil with evil or insult
with insult. On the contrary, repay evil with blessing, because to
this you were called so that you may inherit a blessing.*

1 PETER 3:8–9 NIV

Keep Me Faithful

Lord, when times are hard and I become discouraged, be with me. Keep me a faithful teacher of the Way for the sake of my children and all those to come. May the next generation see You in me, I pray. Amen.

We will not hide them from their descendants; we will tell the next generation the praiseworthy deeds of the LORD, his power, and the wonders he has done.
PSALM 78:4 NIV

I Will Praise You

Just as You rescued Your servant David, You reach
down and rescue me. I will praise You for Your wonderful
creation, for Your steadfast love, and for being the one
true God. Please, Father, let me never tire of giving
You the praise that You are due. Amen.

I will praise you, LORD, among the nations;
I will sing the praises of your name.
2 SAMUEL 22:50 NIV

Sufficient Grace

Father, when I am a poor example to someone I meet, grant me forgiveness. Grant those I offend the wisdom to understand that no one is free of sin, but Your grace is sufficient. Amen.

....
....
....
....
....
....
....
....
....
....
....
....
....
....
....
....

But he said to me, "My grace is sufficient for you, for my power is made perfect in weakness." Therefore I will boast all the more gladly about my weaknesses, so that Christ's power may rest on me.
2 Corinthians 12:9 niv

A Light to My Path

Lord, Your Word is a lamp in my darkness—a flashlight on the path of life that helps me see the way. Your words enlighten me with wisdom, insight, and hope, even when I cannot see where I am going or how things will turn out. Thank You. Amen.

*Your word is a lamp to my feet
and a light to my path.*
PSALM 119:105 NASB

Heaven and Earth

God, Your thoughts are as far above mine as the heavens are above the earth. It is hard for me to fathom that You spoke all of this into existence—the trees and flowers of all kinds, animals in all their uniqueness, even human beings. You have given man so much authority and responsibility in Your world. Help us to be wise stewards of Your creation. Amen.

....

....

....

....

....

....

....

....

....

....

....

....

....

*"Lord, the God of Israel, enthroned between the cherubim,
you alone are God over all the kingdoms of the earth.
You have made heaven and earth."*
2 Kings 19:15 niv

A Joyful Noise

Lord, You are my strength and my song. Help me teach my children to sing, no matter what is going on around us. I want us to make a joyful noise to You, Jesus, the Author and Finisher of our faith. Amen.

Shout joyfully to the LORD, all the earth. Serve the LORD with gladness; come before Him with joyful singing. Know that the LORD Himself is God; it is He who has made us, and not we ourselves; we are His people and the sheep of His pasture.
PSALM 100:1–3 NASB

Self-Control

God, self-control is not one of my strengths, and I need to
work on it. Help me turn things over to You and allow
You to develop self-control in my life. Amen.

....

....

....

....

....

....

....

....

....

....

....

*Now for this very reason also, applying all diligence, in your faith
supply moral excellence, and in your moral excellence, knowledge, and
in your knowledge, self-control, and in your self-control, perseverance,
and in your perseverance, godliness, and in your godliness, brotherly
kindness, and in your brotherly kindness, love. For if these qualities
are yours and are increasing, they render you neither useless nor
unfruitful in the true knowledge of our Lord Jesus Christ.*
2 PETER 1:5–8 NASB

Quiet My Spirit

Lord, there's so much chaos. Quiet my spirit. Let me
close my eyes for a moment and experience Your touch.
My strength comes from You, not from any other source.
Calm me. Keep me anchored in You and Your Spirit. Amen.

*The steadfast of mind You will keep in perfect peace,
because he trusts in You.*
ISAIAH 26:3 NASB

Awesome God

God, the word *awesome* has become so overused in the
society in which I live. We call everything from sports
teams to musical artists "awesome." We say that a certain
type of pizza or a kindness shown by a friend is "awesome."
Help us to be cautious as to what truly leaves us in awe.
You, God, the Creator of all and Redeemer of my
heart. . .You are truly awesome! Amen.

....

....

....

....

....

....

....

....

....

....

....

....

....

*You, God, are awesome in your sanctuary; the God of Israel
gives power and strength to his people. Praise be to God!*
PSALM 68:35 NIV

Angels Watching over Me

Lord, I thank You that You are my true companion—
that I am never alone. You have assigned angels to watch
over and protect me. You have given me Your Holy
Spirit and promised that You are with me always,
even to the very end of the age. Amen.

*For He will give His angels charge concerning you,
to guard you in all your ways.*
PSALM 91:11 NASB

That Wonderful Day

Lord, I know there will come a day when we will be in heaven with You. I look forward to that time, and I thank You for the opportunity to share that time and place with You. Just as the criminal who died on the cross next to Yours, I will be with You in Paradise because I believe in You. What a promise! Amen.

And He said to him, "Truly I say to you, today you shall be with Me in Paradise."
LUKE 23:43 NASB

A Hedge of Protection

Lord, be our strong defense and protect our home.
May this be a place of safety, comfort, and peace.
Guard us from outside forces and protect us from harmful
attacks from within. I pray that the Holy Spirit would put
a hedge of protection around our home and family. Amen.

....
....
....
....
....
....
....
....
....
....
....
....
....
....
....
....

You have always put a wall of protection around him and his home
and his property. You have made him prosper in everything he does.
JOB 1:10 NLT

Joy Even in Trials

Lord, it seems odd to consider trials a joyful thing.
But I pray that my challenges in life, these times of
testing, will lead me to greater perseverance. May that
perseverance finish its work so I will be mature and
complete, on my way to wholeness. Amen.

*"I have told you all this so that you may have peace in me.
Here on earth you will have many trials and sorrows.
But take heart, because I have overcome the world."*
JOHN 16:33 NLT

Unfailing Love

Lord, we humans fail one another. I fail my family. I fail my employer. It just comes with the territory of living in a fallen world. I thank You for Your unfailing love. It is unconditional, and it is the same yesterday, today, and tomorrow. I rejoice as Your child that I can always count on You. Amen.

But I trust in your unfailing love;
my heart rejoices in your salvation.
PSALM 13:5 NIV

Your Word Is Like Rain

Lord, thank You for Your words that speak to my heart
and needs. Your life-giving messages are like rain showers
on new, green grass. I need not just a sprinkle, but a
downpour—a soaking, abundant rain in my dry heart! Amen.

*Let my teaching fall on you like rain; let my speech settle
like dew. Let my words fall like rain on tender grass,
like gentle showers on young plants.*
DEUTERONOMY 32:2 NLT

Sharing the Gift

God, my responsibility as Your child is to share the gift of salvation with others. So many need to hear the Gospel. Make me attentive to each opportunity You present to me. Amen.

Then Jesus came to them and said, "All authority in heaven and on earth has been given to me. Therefore go and make disciples of all nations, baptizing them in the name of the Father and of the Son and of the Holy Spirit, and teaching them to obey everything I have commanded you. And surely I am with you always, to the very end of the age."
MATTHEW 28:18–20 NIV

Secure in Love

Father, I pray I will be able to bear death as well as I bore life, secure in Your love and looking to the salvation that You have promised is mine. Amen.

"Do not let your hearts be troubled. You believe in God; believe also in me. My Father's house has many rooms; if that were not so, would I have told you that I am going there to prepare a place for you? And if I go and prepare a place for you, I will come back and take you to be with me that you also may be where I am."

JOHN 14:1–3 NIV

Confidence

Father, cleanse me from my ungrounded fears. Fill me with
confidence that I can share with my family and friends.
You are the strong Protector. I am thankful that, because of
Jesus, we will be lifted up as the stones in a crown. Amen.

*On that day the LORD their God will rescue his people,
just as a shepherd rescues his sheep. They will
sparkle in his land like jewels in a crown.*
ZECHARIAH 9:16 NLT

Praise the Lord!

Lord, may all creation praise You as I praise You. Amen.

....
....
....
....
....
....
....
....
....
....
....
....
....
....
....
....
....
....

Let every created thing give praise to the LORD, for he issued his command, and they came into being. He set them in place forever and ever. His decree will never be revoked. Praise the LORD from the earth, you creatures of the ocean depths, fire and hail, snow and clouds, wind and weather that obey him, mountains and all hills, fruit trees and all cedars, wild animals and all livestock, small scurrying animals and birds.
PSALM 148:5–10 NLT

The Promise

Thank You for Your promise to guide me in all
things great and small. Your eye is always on me,
keeping me from error and ensuring that I can
always find a way home to You. Amen.

*The LORD is watching everywhere,
keeping his eye on both the evil and the good.*
PROVERBS 15:3 NLT

Saved by Grace

Lord, You give the best gifts! I receive the love
gift of my salvation, knowing that it is by grace
that I have been saved, through faith. I didn't do
anything to deserve it or earn it. Instead, You saved
me by grace so I can now do good works. Amen.

*For it is by grace you have been saved, through faith —
and this is not from yourselves, it is the gift of God —
not by works, so that no one can boast.*
EPHESIANS 2:8–9 NIV

Great Peace

Lord, You have given me a peace that allows me to live confidently in this world. Even if people disagree with my beliefs, even if I am persecuted or belittled, I will rest in Your peace. Nothing has the power to come against me, because I am Your child. I love Your law and I seek to follow it. In Jesus' name, amen.

Great peace have those who love your law,
and nothing can make them stumble.
PSALM 119:165 NIV

Simple Service

Father, there comes a time in every woman's life when
her parents begin to need help. Give me the wisdom to
understand the problems they are having and the often
simple ways I can be of service to them. Amen.

---

*"Honor your father and mother"—which is the first
commandment with a promise—"so that it may go well
with you and that you may enjoy long life on the earth."*
EPHESIANS 6:2–3 NIV

Beyond Beauty

Lord, teach me to look through appearance when I choose my friends. Help me see beyond beauty — or lack of it. It is what is on the inside that counts. Amen.

Rather, it should be that of your inner self, the unfading beauty of a gentle and quiet spirit, which is of great worth in God's sight.
1 PETER 3:4 NIV

God Is Worthy

You created all things, and in You, all things have their being. You are the Creator of the universe. You are worthy of praise and honor. May I never take You for granted or speak to You casually. Yes, You are my Abba Father, but You are also the Sovereign God of the world. You are my King, worthy of more glory and honor than I am capable of giving. Amen.

"You are worthy, our Lord and God, to receive glory and honor and power, for you created all things, and by your will they were created and have their being."

REVELATION 4:11 NIV

Hospitality

Lord, thank You for my home. Show me opportunities to
open this home to others. However my home compares with
others', I thank You for what I have. I am grateful that
Your Spirit is present here. Give me a generous, open heart,
and use my home for Your purposes. Amen.

*Do not neglect to show hospitality to strangers,
for by this some have entertained angels without knowing it.*
HEBREWS 13:2 NASB

Transform My Mind

Lord, sometimes I feel like my emotions need a makeover.
Renovate me—transform me so I can be balanced
and healthy emotionally. I ask for Your power to change.
I don't want to be the way I used to be. I want to be
wise and enjoy sound thinking. Amen.

....
....
....
....
....
....
....
....
....
....
....
....
....
....
....
....

*And we all, who with unveiled faces contemplate the Lord's glory,
are being transformed into his image with ever-increasing glory,
which comes from the Lord, who is the Spirit.*
2 CORINTHIANS 3:18 NIV

A Lighter Heart

Lord, buoy my spirits. I need more joy in my life. Daily living and trials can be so depleting; I just can't do it on my own. Help me to laugh more and enjoy life again. Help me to have a childlike, playful spirit—a lighter heart, Lord. Amen.

" 'You have made known to me the paths of life; you will fill me with joy in your presence.' "
ACTS 2:28 NIV

Nothing Is Impossible

Father, quite often I pray for what is impossible. But for You, nothing is impossible. Even where there seems to be no way, You can make a way. Help me to trust in You to do the impossible in my life. Then, when blessings come, remind me to give You all the honor and glory. In Jesus' name I pray, amen.

"For nothing will be impossible with God."
LUKE 1:37 NASB

Rest

Lord, I need rest. I am so tired and worn out. Help me
sleep well at night. I ask for more energy during the
day and a more vibrant spirit. Lighten my load so I can
have a better balance between my work, ministry,
and home life. Replenish me, Lord. Amen.

_By the seventh day God completed His work which He had done, and
He rested on the seventh day from all His work which He had done._
GENESIS 2:2 NASB

The Future

Lord, thank You for giving me hope. I don't know what the future holds, but You give me the ability to be joyful even while I wait. Please help me to live with a mindset of patience and courage as You work Your will in my life. Amen.

"For I know the plans I have for you," declares the LORD, "plans to prosper you and not to harm you, plans to give you hope and a future."
JEREMIAH 29:11 NIV

Our Nation's Leaders

Lord, we are a hurt nation — an angry nation struggling to maintain its values while still dealing firmly with those who hate us. Guide our nation's leaders during these difficult times. We trust in You and long for peace. Amen.

"You will hear of wars and rumors of wars, but see to it that you are not alarmed. Such things must happen, but the end is still to come."
MATTHEW 24:6 NIV

Never Hesitate to Forgive Others

Lord, may I never hesitate to forgive anyone when
You have already forgiven me. I am so blessed to
be forgiven and made right with You. Amen.

*"Therefore, my friends, I want you to know that through Jesus
the forgiveness of sins is proclaimed to you. Through him
everyone who believes is set free from every sin, a justification
you were not able to obtain under the law of Moses."*
ACTS 13:38–39 NIV

God's Timetable

Father, help me to have patience, knowing my season is coming according to Your timetable and trusting that with Your help, every fruit I produce will be good. Amen.

"For my thoughts are not your thoughts, neither are your ways my ways," declares the LORD. "As the heavens are higher than the earth, so are my ways higher than your ways and my thoughts than your thoughts."

ISAIAH 55:8–9 NIV

Remembering God's Ways

Lord Jesus, I thank You for all the times when You have rescued me. I pray that I will always remember Your ways and walk in them. I desperately need Your help to survive and thrive in this dark world. You are my Helper and my gracious, loving, sovereign God. Amen.

You come to the help of those who gladly do right,
who remember your ways.
ISAIAH 64:5 NIV

God's Roles

Lord, You are called Wonderful Counselor because You freely
give wisdom and guidance. You are the Mighty God, the
One who made the entire world and keeps it all going. My
Everlasting Father, it's Your love and compassion that sustain
me. My Prince of Peace, I worship and honor You. Amen.

*For to us a child is born, to us a son is given, and the government
will be on his shoulders. And he will be called Wonderful Counselor,
Mighty God, Everlasting Father, Prince of Peace.*

ISAIAH 9:6 NIV

The Patience to Wait

Lord, help me to overcome the urge to pat myself on the back in the sight of others. Give me a desire to do good for the sake of doing good and not for praise from those around me. Give me the patience to wait for the day when I will hear You say, "Well done, good and faithful servant." Amen.

....
....
....
....
....
....
....
....
....
....
....
....
....
....
....

Pride goes before destruction,
a haughty spirit before a fall.
PROVERBS 16:18 NIV

Vows

Vows to You must be kept, Father. You not only remember
Your promises to us; You never forget our promises to You.
Help me treat my vows to You seriously, Lord. If sacrifices
are required of me, let me bear them in faith. Amen.

....

....

....

....

....

....

....

....

....

....

....

....

....

....

....

....

You will pray to him, and he will hear you,
and you will fulfill your vows.
JOB 22:27 NIV

Rescue Me

Lord, rescue me from my sea of doubt and fear. I don't want
to be like an ocean wave that is blown and tossed by the
wind. Please quiet my stormy emotions and help me
believe that You will take care of me. Amen.

*Until we all reach unity in the faith and in the knowledge of the Son of
God and become mature, attaining to the whole measure of the fullness
of Christ. Then we will no longer be infants, tossed back and forth by
the waves, and blown here and there by every wind of teaching and by
the cunning and craftiness of people in their deceitful scheming.*
EPHESIANS 4:13–14 NIV

Good Foods

Lord, thank You for filling the earth with a bounty of
food. Help me to make a priority of eating a nutritious
blend of foods, to drink enough water, and to avoid
overindulging in junk. Help me find food that is healthy
and the will to eat in moderation. Amen.

*The land produced vegetation: plants bearing seed according to
their kinds and trees bearing fruit with seed in it according
to their kinds. And God saw that it was good.*
GENESIS 1:12 NIV

Home

Lord, I often make mistakes on the path of life,
losing sight of the trail and calling out for You.
Thank You for finding me, for putting my feet
back on the path and leading me home. Amen.

*Whoever heeds life-giving correction
will be at home among the wise.*
PROVERBS 15:31 NIV

Free Me

God, I often go about my days unaware of the traps that Satan is setting. He would love to see me stumble and fall. He wants to lure Your children away from You. Be my rock and my fortress. Protect me from his evil schemes. Be my refuge, I pray. Amen.

Since you are my rock and my fortress, for the sake of your name lead and guide me. Keep me free from the trap that is set for me, for you are my refuge.
PSALM 31:3–4 NIV

I Will Trust

God, I wake up with anxiety at times. I fear the future, and I want to slow down the hands of time. I remember when I used to live in peace. I had not a worry in the world. As life goes on, I have grown more fearful. Please calm my racing mind and whisper to me a calm assurance that You have everything under control. Thank You, Father. Amen.

_____

_____

_____

_____

_____

_____

_____

_____

_____

_____

_____

_____

_____

_____

When I am afraid, I put my trust in you. In God,
whose word I praise—in God I trust and am not afraid.
PSALM 56:3–4 NIV

Before I Speak

O God, help me think before I speak. Put words of
kindness in my mouth that will build up others instead
of destroying them. I desire to be virtuous. Amen.

....
....
....
....
....
....
....
....
....
....
....
....
....
....

And so blessing and cursing come pouring out of the same mouth.
Surely, my brothers and sisters, this is not right! Does a spring
of water bubble out with both fresh water and bitter water?
Does a fig tree produce olives, or a grapevine produce figs?
No, and you can't draw fresh water from a salty spring.
JAMES 3:10–12 NLT

Daily Needs

Lord, if I trust You for my eternal salvation, why don't I trust You for my daily needs? Like the Israelites who gathered more manna than they needed, I worry about the future instead of trusting You. Instill in me a trust that You will meet each need as it arises. Amen.

Then the LORD said to Moses, "Look, I'm going to rain down food from heaven for you. Each day the people can go out and pick up as much food as they need for that day. I will test them in this to see whether or not they will follow my instructions."

EXODUS 16:4 NLT

Give Joyously

Father, don't let me feel social pressure when giving.
No matter how much or how little I can give, help me
to give joyously and with a cheerful heart. Amen.

....
....
....
....
....
....
....
....
....
....
....
....
....
....

You must each decide in your heart how much to give.
And don't give reluctantly or in response to pressure.
"For God loves a person who gives cheerfully."
2 CORINTHIANS 9:7 NLT

Harvest of Righteousness

Lord, plant Your wisdom in me like seeds in the soil. Help me cultivate each one and follow Your ways. They are pure, peace-loving, considerate, submissive, full of mercy and good fruit, impartial, and sincere. May I be a person who sows in peace and raises a harvest of righteousness. Amen.

*Peacemakers who sow in peace
reap a harvest of righteousness.*
JAMES 3:18 NIV

Words of Peace and Comfort

Lord, the next time I am angry, guide me away from
sin until I can speak words of peace and comfort once
again. Give me the strategies I need in order to refrain
from sinning when I am angry. I want to be kind
even when I am frustrated. Amen.

*"I hope I continue to please you, sir," she replied.
"You have comforted me by speaking so kindly to me,
even though I am not one of your workers."*
RUTH 2:13 NLT

The Power to Set Things Right

Lord, when my family is treated unfairly or when someone judges me before knowing the whole story, I want to see justice done. Remind me to rely on You for that justice. Only You have the power to set things right once and for all. Amen.

....

....

....

....

....

....

....

....

....

....

....

....

....

....

....

"For I am ready to set things right, not in the distant future, but right now! I am ready to save Jerusalem and show my glory to Israel."
ISAIAH 46:13 NLT

Angels

Heavenly Father, the world is a frightening place. I look
around and see endless opportunities for disaster and
tragedy. And yet, I place my trust in Your promise to
send Your angels to watch over and guard me.
Thank You for Your protection. Amen.

*"And he will send his angels with a loud trumpet call,
and they will gather his elect from the four winds,
from one end of the heavens to the other."*
MATTHEW 24:31 NIV

Cleanse Me

Father, on my worst days I feel totally unworthy.
But I know You have promised to cleanse me from
all unrighteousness, to wipe away my guilt and
make me whole if I confess my sins. Amen.

*"I will cleanse them from all the sin they have committed against
me and will forgive all their sins of rebellion against me."*
JEREMIAH 33:8 NIV

Turning from Sin

Father, remind me often of the need for self-control, so I don't give in to the temptation of sin. Only when we turn from sin can we truly gain understanding in all wisdom. I ask for Your strength to help in this. Amen.

"Therefore, you Israelites, I will judge each of you according to your own ways, declares the Sovereign LORD. Repent! Turn away from all your offenses; then sin will not be your downfall."
EZEKIEL 18:30 NIV

Sheep of His Pasture

Thank You, Lord, for Your love and faithfulness to us.
Thank You for making us Your people and for allowing us
to be the sheep of Your pasture. Thank You for allowing us
to serve such a great God! I will teach Your ways to others.
It is my deep desire that my family will praise Your name
from generation to generation. Amen.

_____

_____

_____

_____

_____

_____

_____

_____

_____

_____

_____

_____

_____

_____

*Then we your people, the sheep of your pasture, will thank you forever
and ever, praising your greatness from generation to generation.*
PSALM 79:13 NLT

Fill Me, Lord

Lord, I am weary. Infuse me with life, energy, and joy
again. I don't have to look to a bowl of ice cream or the
compliments of a friend to fill me up on the inside. Steady
and constant, You are the one who fills me. Amen.

*Oh, how generous and gracious our Lord was! He filled
me with the faith and love that come from Christ Jesus.*
1 TIMOTHY 1:14 NLT

A New Name

Thank You, Father God, that You reached down and saved me from myself. I was on the road to nowhere. Just as You did with Saul, You made Yourself known to me at just the right time. You have given me a new name. I am a child of the Living God. I thank You, Father, for casting my sin away as far as the east is from the west and remembering it no more! Amen.

Do not remember the sins of my youth and my rebellious ways; according to your love remember me, for you, LORD, are good.
PSALM 25:7 NIV

Simple Joys from Above

Lord, thank You for the gift of laughter! Thank You
for the joy You bring into my life through a child's
smile, a luscious peach, a hot bath, a good night's sleep.
Help me remember that when I am "looking up" to You,
I can have a more optimistic outlook. Amen.

*Every good and perfect gift is from above,
coming down from the Father of the heavenly lights,
who does not change like shifting shadows.*
JAMES 1:17 NIV

You Might Also Enjoy. . .

Bible Promise Book® for Women Prayer Edition

Where can women turn when they need God's thoughts on the issues and emotions of life? *The Bible Promise® Book for Women — Prayer Edition*, brand-new as a paperback expanded edition.
Paperback / 978-1-63409-947-9 / $9.99

The Prayers of the Bible Devotional

You can learn much from the faith-filled, desperate, hopeful, even selfish prayers in scripture — and you'll find great insights in *The Prayers of the Bible Devotional*.
Paperback / 978-1-63058-908-0 / $5.99